American Quilter's Society

MW00355871

YEARS

CATALOGUE OF
SHOW QUILTS

2019 EDITION

AQS QuiltWeek® Show – Spring - Paducah
Semifinalists

Includes 35 Years of Best of Show Winners

Located in Paducah, Kentucky, the American Quilter's Society (AQS) is dedicated to promoting the accomplishments of today's quilters. Through its publications and events, AQS strives to honor today's quiltmakers and their work and to inspire future creativity and innovation in quiltmaking.

Artwork © 2019, American Quilter's Society

EDITOR: BONNIE K. BROWNING
GRAPHIC DESIGN: LYNDA SMITH
CONTENT EDITOR: HANNAH ALTON AND ANDREA RAY
COVER DESIGN: DREW JOHNSON
PHOTOGRAPHY: SUPPLIED BY THE INDIVIDUAL QUILTMAKERS

American Quilter's Society
PO Box 3290 • Paducah, KY 42002-3290
Fax 270-898-1173 • e-mail: orders@AQSquilt.com

Additional copies of this book may be ordered from the American Quilter's Society, PO Box 3290, Paducah, KY 42002-3290, or online at www.AmericanQuilter.com.

Proudly printed and bound in the United States of America

Paducah photos courtesy of Paducah Visitors Bureau.

AQS celebrates 35 years of presenting the work of today's talented quilters at AQS QuiltWeek® – Spring Paducah, Kentucky 2019.

AQS QuiltWeek events are the place to meet your friends, learn from top national and international quilt instructors, have fun at special events, and shop for the latest machines and supplies in the Merchant Mall.

Quilters representing 44 states and 16 countries will be displayed in this year's contest. Techniques used in the 410 quilts juried into the contest represent traditional appliqué, piecing, and quilting by hand and machine, and they also include innovative techniques like painting, thread painting, and a wide variety of embellishments.

Have you entered your quilts in an AQS show? Now there are more opportunities for you to enter—you could win part of the $463,000 available in the 2019 AQS quilt contests.

We hope to see an entry from you in the future.

Meredith Schroeder

Meredith Schroeder
AQS President and Cofounder

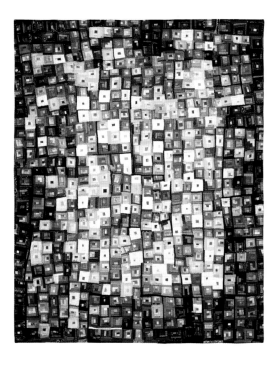

101. LIGHT OF PEACE, 70" x 90"
Eunjoo An, Yongin, Gyeonggi, South Korea

102. FROM THE INSIDE OUT, 95" x 95"
Catherine Butterworth
Lindfield, New South Wales, Australia

103. MY SPLENDID SAMPLER—FIRST GENERATION
104" x 104"
Janet Dalis, Melrose, MA

104. RAINBOW KALEIDOSCOPES, 71" x 93"
Dorinda Evans and Ingrid Whitcher, Madison, MS

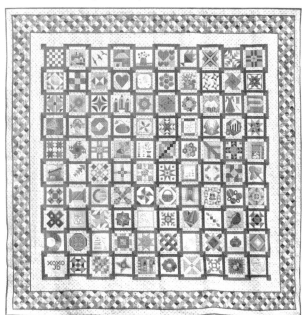

The Splendid Sampler: 100 Spectacular Blocks from a Community of Quilters by Pat Sloan and Jane Davidson © 2017 That Patchwork Place

Arcadia Avenue pattern by Shayla and Kristy Wolf, Sassafras Lane Designs

The Caswell Quilt pattern by Corliss Searcey, Threadbear Patchwork & Quilting

105. RHAPSODY IN BLACK, 86" x 86"
Mark F. Glover, Sequim, WA

106. CASWELL PLUS, 83" x 95"
Karen L. Guthrie, Marshall, MO

107. FEELS LIKE SPRING, 81" x 105"
Susan Kadlubar and Michelle Jones
North Little Rock, AR

108. A SEA OF CLOUDS—SPRING, 78" x 87"
Keiko Morita, Toyama, Toyama, Japan

Feels Like Spring pattern by Smith Street Designs

109. Eternal Beauty, 95" x 95"
Sherry Reynolds, Laramie, WY

110. Oh Be Joyful!, 74" x 92"
Cindy Seitz-Krug, Overgaard, AZ

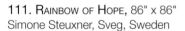

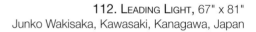

111. Rainbow of Hope, 86" x 86"
Simone Steuxner, Sveg, Sweden

112. Leading Light, 67" x 81"
Junko Wakisaka, Kawasaki, Kanagawa, Japan

201. TROPICAL VACATION, 94" x 94"
Amy Allen, Honaunau, HI

202. BETWEEN BLACK AND WHITE, 90" x 90"
Karen Bean and Sherrie Coppenbarger, Waltonville, IL

203. CAIRN, 98" x 108"
Teri Biglands, Peachtree City, GA

204. KYNDRAH'S WONDERLAND, 80" x 80"
May Black, Rolla, MO

3 Shades of Gray pattern by Carolyn Burgess Hughey, Quilter's Newsletter © 2014

Allisyn's Wondered Land pattern by Judy and Bradley Niemeyer, Quiltworx.com

Vintage Quilt Revival: 22 Modern Designs from Classic Blocks by Katie Clark Blakesley, Lee Heinrich, and Faith Jones © 2013 Interweave

Friends of Baltimore pattern by Susan H. Garman, Come Quilt LLC

205. VINTAGE QUILT REVIVAL, 80" x 96"
Jan Daoust, Montrose, CO

206. FRIENDS OF BALTIMORE MEET SOUTH TEXAS
85" x 85"
Kathleen Dombi, Weslaco, TX

207. MOONLIGHT GARDEN, 90" x 90"
Sherry Durbin, Burnsville, NC

208. ANOTHER TIME AND PLACE, 83" x 83"
Robbi Joy Eklow, Omaha, NE

209. THE GRAPE QUILT, 84" x 84"
Jerrianne Evans, Houston, TX

210. THE LOYAL UNION SAMPLER—FROM ELM CREEK QUILT, 97" x 96"
Karin Galvão, Salvador, Bahia, Brazil

211. HAMPTON RIDGE, 93" x 93"
Susan Goodley, Rock Island, IL

212. A DIFFERENT TAKE ON MOON GLOW CANDLELIGHT, 90" x 90"
Frieda Grischkowsky, Stillwater, OK

213. LUCY BOSTON GALLERY, 87" x 87"
Bette Haddon and Marcia Henry, Pearland, TX

214. ASHLEY'S AMISH, 96" x 100"
Barb Heetland, Milford, IA

215. HUES, 92" x 92"
Shari Novak Johnson, Lawrence, KS

216. PANAMA PYRAMIDS, 73" x 88"
Donna Karolus, Cleveland, WI

217. Covered in Leaves, 65" x 91"
Susan Kelley, Hallsville, MO

Stars in His Crown pattern by Robert Callaham, *McCall's Quilting*

218. Stars in His Crown, 84" x 84"
Marilyn Lidstrom Larson, Willow City, ND

219. Dimensional Explosion, 88" x 100"
Diane Lehman, Badger, IA

220. Aegean Sea by Judy Martin, 98" x 98"
Holly Lewis, Cottage Grove, MN

A Prairie Gathering pattern by Pam Buda, Heartspun Quilts

Stellar Quilts by Judy Martin © 2018 C&T Publishing / Crosley-Griffith

221. MY HOMAGE TO RED & GREEN QUILTS, 85" x 84"
Jan Lewis and Tammy Oberlin, Grand Rapids, MI

222. TWIST OF FLOWERS, 88" x 89"
Anne Lillholm, Nuenen, Noord-Brabant, Netherlands

223. MODERN DAY WEDDING RING QUILT
107" x 107"
Judith Malinowski, Canton, OH

224. HALO MEDALLION, 86" x 86"
Karen Maloley, Richmond, KY

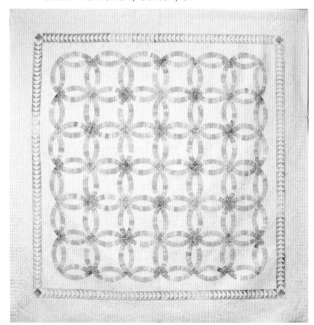

Large Quilts – Movable Machine Quilted

225. ANDROMEDA CROSSING, 83" x 83"
Karen Marchetti, Port St. Lucie, FL

226. LADY IN RED, 104" x 104"
Shari McDonnell-Guimont and Marlene Hiltner
Duluth, MN

227. PANDEMONIUM, 92" x 92"
Susan Minchow, Pleasant Dale, NE

228. SEASONS OF LIFE, 83" x 83"
Sandra Mollon and Kris Spray, Valley Springs, CA

Lady of 10,000 Lakes pattern by Claudia Clark Myers, Claudia Myers Designs

Pandemonium pattern by Kim McLean, Glorious Color

Art and craft designs of the early and late 19th and early 20th centuries

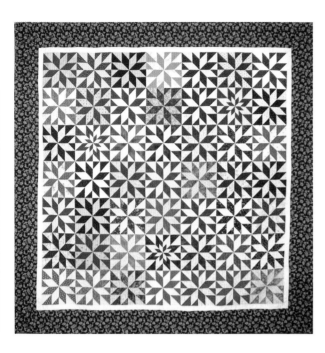

229. PINWHEEL STARS, 83" x 83"
Emmy Adrian Moore and Nancy Adrian Smith
Decatur, IL

230. SNAKE RIVER LOG CABIN, 93" x 93"
Carolyn Bucklin Mullins, Daniels, WV

231. YOUR PLACE OR MINE, 81" x 81"
Marva-Lee Otos, Ketchikan, AK

232. ANCIENT STARS, 67" x 90"
Debby Porter and Alicia Edwards, Casper, WY

Fair Isles Winter BOM by Reeze L. Hanson, Morning Glory Designs

233. THE BIRDS AND THE BEES, 71" x 82"
Beckey Prior, Henderson, TX

234. FAIR ISLES WINTER, 87" x 87"
Gail H. Smith and Angela McCorkle
North Barrington, IL

235. FLOWER POWER, 80" x 102"
Ron Stefanak and John Anderson, Fulton, NY

236. SPOT ON!, 86" x 86"
Gail Stepanek and Jan Hutchison, New Lenox, IL

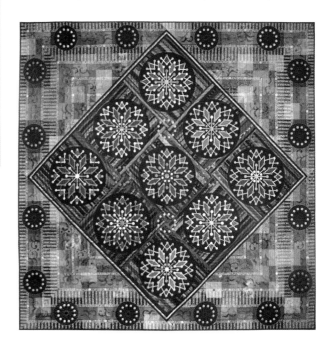

Large Quilts – Movable Machine Quilted
Large Quilts – 1st Entry in an AQS Paducah Quilt Contest

Celebrating Mary Brown pattern by Corliss Searcey, Threadbear Patchwork & Quilting

Dover clip art and Indian henna tattoos

237. CELEBRATING MARY BROWN, 86" x 86"
Christine Sudberry, Tampa, FL

238. KARMA CHAMELEON, 69" x 81"
Kris Vierra, Lincoln, NE

301. RIVER MOVEMENT, 95" x 95"
Wendy Ahnen, Eagle River, WI

302. TABER-WELBORN FAMILY TREE QUILT, 83" x 89"
Sue Atlas, Lakeside, CA

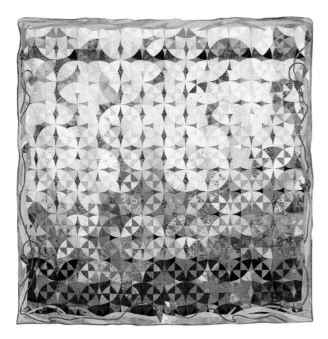

Early American Design Motifs by Suzanne E. Chapman and American Folk Art Designs & Motifs for Artists and Craftspeople by Joseph D'Addetta © 2003 and 2011 Dover Publications

Holiday Blessings pattern from *Traditions from Elm Creek Quilts: 13 Quilt Projects to Piece and Appliqué* by Jennifer Chiaverini © 2011 C&T Publishing

303. CONNECT HEARTS, 76" x 90"
Noriko Atobe, Saku, Nagano, Japan

304. SECOND TIME AROUND, 65" x 82"
Cynthia Waters Barton, St. Louis, MO

305. YELLOW FEVER, 73" x 87"
Janice H. Black, Ringgold, GA

306. BIRDS AND THE BEE, 75" x 86"
Nancy B. Blake, Madison, WI

Hummingbird design by Patricia Cox, Morning Glory's Light pattern by Cindy Taylor Clark, Songbirds in My Garden pattern by Joan Jones, and *Fifty Favorite Birds Coloring Book* by Lisa Bonforte © 1982 Dover Publications

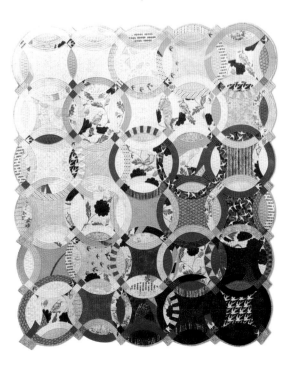

Victoria Findlay Wolfe Double Wedding Ring templates and workshop

Love Entwined pattern by Esther Aliu

School and apple designs by Lori Holt, Bee In My Bonnet

307. 1790 Love Entwined, 97" x 97"
Marlee Carter, New Gloucester, ME

308. All About You, 84" x 84"
Dianne Craig, Rogersville, AL

309. Barnum & Bailey, 105" x 105"
Daisy Dodge, Carmel, NY

310. Toy Box, 84" x 80"
Jill Doscher and Julia Graziano, Skaneateles, NY

Ossanna Quilt pattern by Meg Callahan

311. FIORI DELLA NONNA, 77" x 80"
Elis Marina Sehnem Engels
Taio, Santa Catarina, Brazil

312. ARIZONA MINING, 88" x 88"
Kerry Fisbeck, Edmond, OK

313. FESTIVAL OF STARS, 74" x 81"
Connie Hansen, Hamilton, TX

314. ANNIVERSARY, 87" x 87"
Michiyo Hashimoto, Seto, Aichi, Japan

Festival of Stars pattern by Sue Harvey and Sandy Boobar, Pine Tree Country Quilts

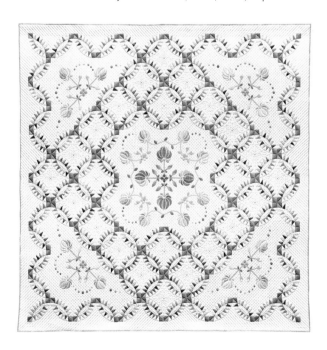

American Heritage pattern by Julia Hale, Bits 'n Pieces

Getting to Know Hue pattern by Nancy Rink, Nancy Rink Designs

315. STARS AND STRIPES, 75" x 82"
Sue Horton and Linda Potter, Golden, MO

316. COLOR EXPLOSION, 95" x 100"
Cindy Hoste, Geneseo, IL

317. REINCARNATION, 63" x 86"
Takako Ikuno, Yokohama, Kanagawa, Japan

318. ULTRAVIOLET JANE, 83" x 83"
Christa Johnston, Jefferson City, MO

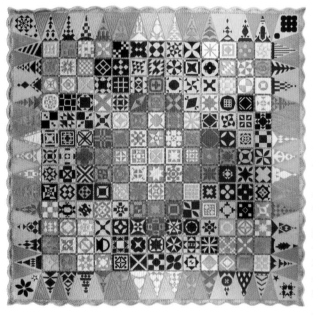

Dear Jane: The Two Hundred Twenty-five Patterns from the 1863 Jane A. Stickle Quilt by Brenda Manges Papadakis © 1996 Quilt House Publishing

Pathway to the Stars pattern by Roxanne Carter, Quilting With Roxanne

319. A‍MAZZING G‍RACE, 108" x 108"
Shari Jones, Sun City West, AZ

320. R‍AINBOW S‍UPERNOVA, 97" x 93"
Dana Kuhnline, Cincinnati, OH

321. A‍LMOST B‍LACK AND W‍HITE S‍AMPLER,
89" x 110"
JoAnne Lammert, St. Louis, MO

322. M‍ENNONITE L‍ONE S‍TAR, 97" x 97"
Patricia Loux, Morris, PA

Orange You Sweet pattern by Gina Gempesaw, Fons & Porter's Love of Quilting

Vintage quilt from Mennonite Heritage Center, Harleysville, PA

323. KARMA, 105" x 110"
Gul Mahmutoğlu, Ankara, Turkey

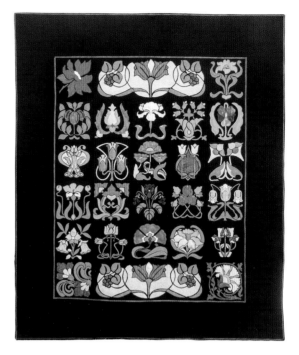

Deco Garden BOM by Reeze L. Hanson, Morning Glory Designs

324. ART NOUVEAU, 76" x 89"
Heather Mantz, Troy, IL

325. CIRCLE JUBILEE, 88" x 88"
Becky McDaniel, Laguna Niguel, CA

326. TRIPLE DIAMONDS, 90" x 95"
Brianne Moores, Sequim, WA

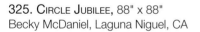

Circle Jubilee pattern by Pam Clarke, Fons and Porter's Love of Quilting July/August 2006

Reaching Out pattern by Edyta Sitar, Laundry Basket Quilts

Patches of Blue: 17 Quilt Patterns and a Gallery of Inspiring Antique Quilts by Edyta Sitar © 2017 Laundry Basket Quilts

327. OLD VINE ZEN, 68" x 83"
Tracey Moyer, Shillington, PA

328. BLUE FOREST, 73" x 93"
Shizue Naito, Toyohashi, Aichi, Japan

329. EARLY SUMMER WITH FRESH BREEZE, 67" x 83"
Setsuko Oki, Narita, Chiba, Japan

330. MOTHER DAUGHTER QUILT, 81" x 90"
Karen Penrod and Jennifer Benne, Parma, MI

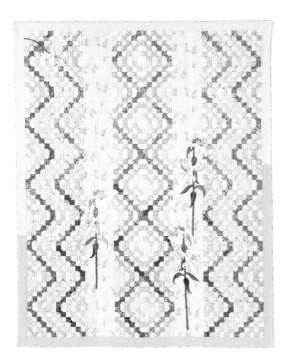

Ashley's Flower Basket pattern and Jessica's Flower Basket pattern by Sue Nickels

Mixing Quilt Elements: A Modern Look at Color, Style & Design by Kathy Doughty © 2016 C&T Publishing

Pandemonium pattern by Kim McLean, Glorious Color

331. FAIRY TALE GARDEN, 66" x 80"
Sherrie Plowman, Geneva, IL

332. PANDEMONIUM, 88" x 84"
Gale Polk and Julie Lillo, Stevensville, MI

333. RUFFLED ROSES, 86" x 86"
Kim Radabaugh, Twin Falls, ID

334. COXCOMB NOUVEAU, 80" x 81"
Wilma Richter and Leah Sample, Little Rock, AR

Ruffled Roses pattern by Susan H. Garman, Come Quilt LLC

Coxcomb Quilt (Your First Quilt Book) by Donna Hanson Eines © 1998 Martingale & Co and Fabulous Background Quilting for Appliqué iquilt class by Judi Madsen

The Caswell Quilt pattern by Corliss Searcey, Threadbear Patchwork & Quilting

335. THE CASWELL QUILT, 68" x 80"
Roberta Schmitz, Edwardsville, KS

Old-fashioned appliqué quilt patterns by Kumiko Fujita

336. MY BALTIMORE ALBUM QUILT, 91" x 91"
Hyun Jung Shin, Seoul, South Korea

337. THE POWER OF PINK, 70" x 88"
Judy Soedt, Blue Grass, IA

338. REMINISCENCE, 81" x 90"
Mariko Takeda, Nagoya, Aichi, Japan

Scrap Happy Sampler BOM by Sherri Noel, Modern Quilting by Sherri Noel

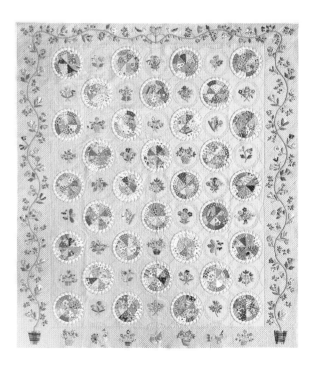

339. MILLEFIORE, 92" x 92"
Karen Vosen, Havre, MT

340. MY JOURNEY, 87" x 103"
Judy Waln, Golden, CO

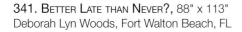

341. BETTER LATE THAN NEVER?, 88" x 113"
Deborah Lyn Woods, Fort Walton Beach, FL

401. RUBY WEDDING ANNIVERSARY, 78" x 78"
Harumi Asada, Higashiura, Chita, Aichi, Japan

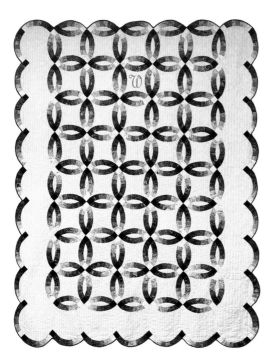

402. WHITE-TAILED STAR, 88" x 88"
Betty Lu Brydges, Nobleboro, ME

403. FLOWER FESTIVAL, 79" x 78"
Sachiko Chiba, Morioka, Iwate, Japan

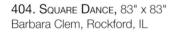

404. SQUARE DANCE, 83" x 83"
Barbara Clem, Rockford, IL

405. WEDGEWOOD, 75" x 87"
Donna French Collins, Pennellville, NY

406. Ocean Coral, 72" x 72"
Daisy Dodge, Carmel, NY

407. Numquam Cede, 96" x 96"
Elisabeth Frolet, Dunwoody, GA

408. Cats & Stars, 75" x 79"
Yukie Fujitomi, Chiba, Chiba, Japan

409. In Season, 72" x 72"
Miyuki Hamaba, Sanda, Hyogo, Japan

410. JINGLE BELLS, 65" x 52"
Antonia Hering, Hoorn, Noord-Holland, Netherlands

411. THE DAYS SPENT WITH BALTIMORE, 83" x 83"
Toshiko Imai, Sagamihara, Kagawa, Japan

412. LE BOUQUET, 81" x 81"
Mayumi Ishii, Tokorozawa, Saitama, Japan

413. MAU LOA (EVERLASTING), 83" x 83"
Joyce Johnson, Augusta, MO

414. Past and Future Meet, 86" x 86"
Noriko Kido, Azumino, Nagano, Japan

415. Colourful Retina, 87" x 87"
Sugy Kim, Point Cook, Victoria, Australia

416. Blossoms from the East, 90" x 94"
Barbara Korengold, Chevy Chase, MD

417. Elegant Rose Garden, 78" x 78"
Taeko Kozuka, Tokyo, Tokyo, Japan

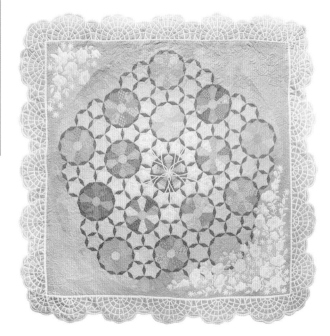

Les Fleurs du Jardin pattern by Lisa DeBee Schiller

418. SUMMER GARDEN, 64" x 74"
Kazumi Matsuo, Kawabe, Hyogo, Japan

419. FLOWERS FROM MY GARDEN, 68" x 86"
Jimmie Ann McLean, Grand Chenier, LA

420. ROSES IN HOMETOWN'S PARK, 78" x 78"
Toyoko Nakajima, Kiryu, Gunma, Japan

421. BOTTOM OF THE BASKET, 88" x 88"
Darla Orndorff, Chandler, AZ

422. Joy in the Journey, 74" x 90"
Lahala Phelps, Washington, UT

423. Little Brown Bird, 84" x 85"
Shirley Milne Prince, Tunnel Hill, GA

424. Child's Game, 60" x 74"
Maria Reuter, Fürstenfeldbruck, Germany

425. Roseville Album, 87" x 87"
Linda Riesterer, Wenatchee, WA

Appliqué Masterpiece: Little Brown Bird Patterns by Margaret Docherty © 1999 American Quilter's Society

Roseville Album, Vases, Birds, and Other Things pattern by Kim McLean, Glorious Color

Baskets & Flowers: Rhapsody Quilts; Design Companion Vol. 2 to Ricky Tims' Rhapsody Quilts Full-Size Freezer Paper Pattern Bonus Appliqué Designs & Ideas by Ricky Tims © 2008 C&T Publishing; Celtic Style Floral Appliqué Designs Using Interlaced Scrollwork by Scarlett Rose © 1995 American Quilter's Society; and Easy Kaleidoscope Stained Glass Coloring Book by A. G. Smith © 2005 Dover Publications

426. HEXAGON II, 88" x 92"
Fumie Sasaki, Rifu, Miyagi, Japan

427. BIZARRO, 87" x 87"
Barbara Shiffler, Matthews, NC

428. WRAPPED WITH SEPIA COLORS, 74" x 74"
Toshie Shimamura, Koshigaya, Saitama, Japan

429. POLISH POTTERY, 74" x 74"
Chieko Shiraishi, Saitama, Saitama, Japan

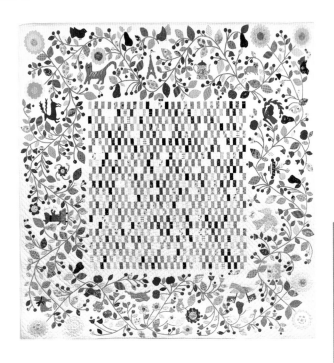

430. THE GOOD BOY QUILT, 88" x 88"
Laurie Simpson, Ann Arbor, MI

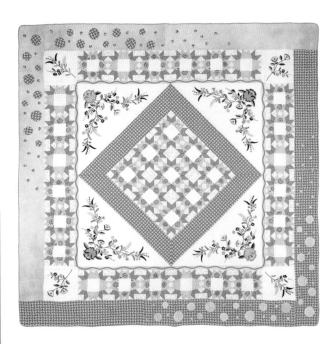

431. ATTRACTED TO KALOCSA EMBROIDERY, 73" x 73"
Sechiko Suzuki, Iwaki, Fukushima, Japan

432. BALTIMORE ALBUM QUILT, 91" x 91"
Akiko Takahashi, Niigata, Niigata, Japan

433. PINWHEEL, 75" x 75"
Noriko Takahashi, Nakano, Tokyo, Japan

434. I WAS IN LOVE AT ONCE, 80" x 80"
Kyouko Tashiro, Shirakawa, Fukushima, Japan

435. FRANCES FLACK'S FIND ANEW, 108" x 108"
Sheri Thompson, Fulton, MD

436. ALICE'S POT OF FLOWERS, 78" x 78"
Alice Tignor, Severna Park, MD

437. DISTANT MEMORY, 79" x 79"
Kazue Tsukayama, Kaga, Ishikawa, Japan

438. ESPALIER, 72" x 79"
Joann Webb, Grain Valley, MO

439. MY CRAZY FAMILY ALBUM, 80" x 80"
Sherry Werum, Woodland, CA

440. BOBBY'S GARDEN, 99" x 99"
Nancy Zachik, Potomac, MD

501. HEART OF THE SEA, 64" x 75"
Lys Axelson, Big Bear City, CA

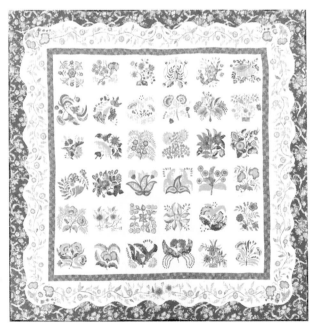

Zeruah's Legacy pattern by Barbara Korengold

Embroidery & Patchwork Revisited: An Illustrated Guide to Hand Stitching by Janice Vaine © 2014 Janice Vaine and Landauer Publishing, an imprint of Fox Chapel Publishing, Inc., www.foxchapelpublishing.com. and An Embroiderers Garden: Floral Collection for Hand Embroidery by Maria Diaz © 2015 Tuva Publishing

502. EVERLASTING, 68" x 68"
Helen Williams Butler, Alpine, UT

503. ANN'S LEGACY, 67" x 67"
Marlee Carter, New Gloucester, ME

504. POLITICAL CIRCUS, 96" x 68"
Misty M. Cole, Bowie, MD

505. REFLECTIONS OF LOVE, 70" x 77"
Jennifer Horsford, Proserpine, Queensland, Australia

506. CONNECTIONS, 72" x 50"
Beth Porter Johnson, Tullahoma, TN

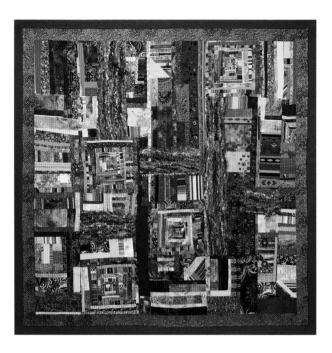

507. BUTTONS FOR BLUE BOY, 62" x 64"
Michele Lea, Oxford, OH

508. LA MODE—MON PRÉFÉRÉ, 66" x 66"
Mariko Miwa, Musashino, Tokyo, Japan

509. STRANGER, 62" x 66"
Chizuko Otsuka, Toyama, Toyama, Japan

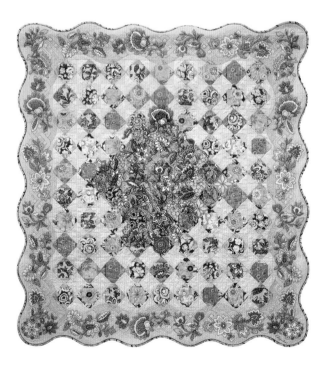

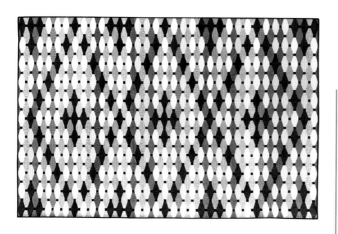

510. TRANQUIL SPACES 3, 80" x 52"
Loretta Painter, Norris, TN

511. REMEMBRANCE, 68" x 68"
Catherine Palmer, Bethlehem, PA

512. CELTIC MIGRATION, 75" x 75"
Angela Petrocelli, Prescott Valley, AZ

513. MEADOW, 72" x 72"
Debra Ramsey, Lexington, OH

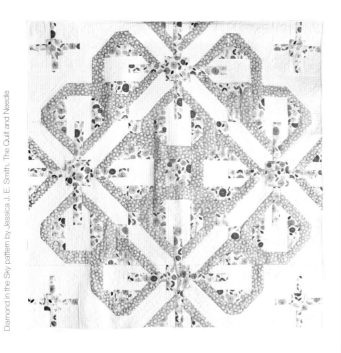

Diamond in the Sky pattern by Jessica J. E. Smith, The Quilt and Needle

514. MID-CENTURY MOD, 60" x 60"
Patricia Roland, Bend, OR

515. KAZENOBON, 67" x 80"
Masako Sakagami, Toyama, Toyama, Japan

516. UKKONKO—TULIP, 71" x 71"
Sachiko Sasakura, Nakano, Tokyo, Japan

517. ENCHANTMENT, 77" x 77"
Berniece Sayer
Mermaid Waters, Queensland, Australia

Bed of Roses pattern by Susan H. Garman, Come Quilt LLC

Vogue Colors A to Z: A Fashion Coloring Book by Valerie Steiker © 2016 Alfred A. Knopf

Flower Box pattern by Edyta Sitar, Laundry Basket Quilts

518. FASHION IN ART DECO, 75" x 68"
Nancy Shiner, Batavia, IL

519. FARM MARKET BLOOMS, 74" x 74"
Nancy Simmons, Duncannon, PA

520. NIGHT SUN, 62" x 62"
Sandi Snow, Lutz, FL

521. MUTTONS & BUTTONS & PEARLS, OH MY!
65" x 71"
Janet Stone, Overland Park, KS

Audrey III pattern by Deb Karasik

522. PEPPERMINT & ROSES, 65" x 65"
Rahna L. Summerlin, Port Orange, FL

523. THE CREATION AND EXPANSION OF THE CUBIC QUILTIVERSE, 68" x 68"
Roger Winchell, Asheville, NC

601. VAN GOGH GALAXY, 62" x 62"
Ellen Ault, Tampa, FL

602. MARIE'S TREASURE, 77" x 77"
Marilyn Badger, St. George, UT

Technicolor Galaxy BOM by Alyssa Lichner, Pile O' Fabric

603. Five Roses, 68" x 67"
Marilyn Farquhar, Heidelberg, Ontario, Canada

604. Seed Pods, 63" x 63"
Linda Fleschner, North Fond du Lac, WI

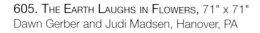

605. The Earth Laughs in Flowers, 71" x 71"
Dawn Gerber and Judi Madsen, Hanover, PA

606. My Secret Garden, 71" x 71"
Margaret Solomon Gunn, Gorham, ME

607. FLOWER GARDEN KALEIDOSCOPE, 74" x 74"
Bette Haddon and Marcia Henry, Pearland, TX

608. GLASS REFLECTIONS, 70" x 55"
Jessica Harper, Hurst, TX

609. MY SPECIAL ROSE, 72" x 72"
Julie Harris, Paducah, KY

610. MEMORIES, 77" x 85"
Joyce Hite and Patricia Hechler, Springboro, OH

Vintage Rose pattern by Judy and Bradley Niemeyer, Quiltworx.com

138 Original Applique Designs by Yoko Saito © 2016 Stitch Publications

611. STARS GALORE, 71" x 76"
Meg Latimer, Alpharetta, GA

612. DIAMONDS BARGELLO, 65" x 71"
Holly Lewis, Cottage Grove, MN

613. GRANDMA'S CANDY JAR, 77" x 77"
Beth Markel, Rochester, MI

614. ALL YOUR FAVORITE SONGS, 67" x 67"
Judy Martin and Dawn Cavanaugh, Grinnell, IA

WILL BENNETT & THE TELLS

ALL YOUR FAVORITE SONGS

The New Hexagon - Millefiore Quilt-Along by Katja Marek

615. THIS IS YOUR BRAIN ON KAFFE, 78" x 78"
Sherry Massey, Edmond, OK

616. JANE SASSAMAN'S GARDEN, 70" x 70"
Ann Matheson, Mount Dora, FL

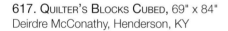

617. QUILTER'S BLOCKS CUBED, 69" x 84"
Deirdre McConathy, Henderson, KY

618. CIRCLE OF LIFE, 65" x 65"
Jan McCreary, Wichita, KS

Circle of Life pattern by Jacqueline de Jonge. BeColourful.com

619. IN FULL BLOOM, 69" x 83"
Claudia Pfeil, Krefeld, Germany

620. GEOMETRY. CALIENTE!, 72" x 72"
Suzanne Reiter, Tarpon Springs, FL

Karen K. Stone Quilts by Karen K. Stone © 2004 The Electric Quilt Company

621. STARS CAN'T SHINE WITHOUT DARKNESS
79" x 81", Claudia Scheja
Werne, North Rhine-Westphalia, Germany

622. BALTIMORE CHRISTMAS, 66" x 66"
Marilla Schmitt, Cottage Grove, MN

Baltimore Christmas pattern by Pearl P. Pereira, P3 Designs

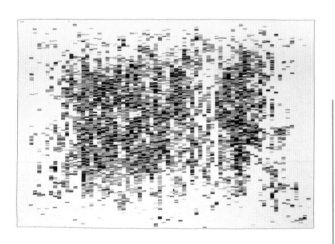

623. ALPINE MEADOW, 74" x 49"
Cynthia L. Vogt, Kennewick, WA

624. SILK BEAUTY, 79" x 79"
Karen Vosen, Havre, MT

The Rose of Sharon Block Book: Winning Designs from the EQ6 Challenge by Sharon Pederson © 2010 That Patchwork Place, blocks designed by Carolyn Laukkonen, and Beautiful Botanicals: 45 Appliqué Flowers & 14 Quilt Projects by Deborah Kemball © 2011 C&T Publishing

625. HEXIE GLITTER, 69" x 78"
Nancy Wheatley, Creal Springs, IL

701. SEA BREEZE, 60" x 41"
Joanne Baeth, Bonanza, OR

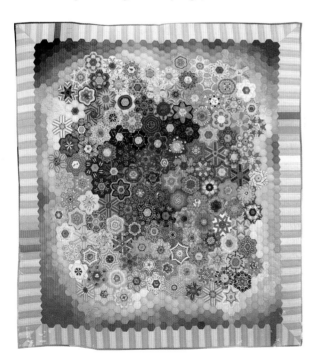

702. THROUGH MY FATHER'S EYES, 64" x 41"
Amy Cavaness, Marseilles, IL

703. STEPPING UP, 65" x 54"
Pat Durbin, Arcata, CA

704. DESTINY MANIFESTED, 96" x 54"
Laura Fogg, Ukiah, CA

705. ON REFLECTION, 67" x 40"
Jan Frazer, Elwood, Victoria, Australia

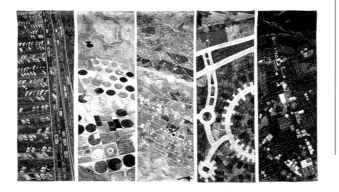

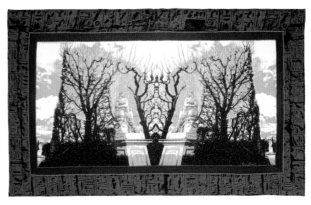

Reece Scannell screen print fabric

Wall Quilts – Pictorial

706. SAN FRANCISCO FIREBOAT, 70" x 56"
Diane Long, Lena, IL

707. BELOVED TREE, 60" x 66"
Katherine Ludington, Boston, MA

708. LITTLE ARTISTS, 67" x 65"
Hiroko Miyama and Masanobu Miyama
Azumino, Nagano, Japan

709. POWER, 71" x 51"
Inez Rovegno, Crane Hill, AL

Inlayed marble floor of the Cathedral of Siena, Italy

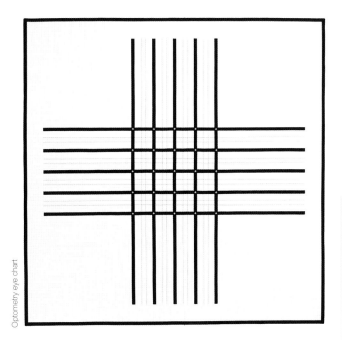

Optometry eye chart

801. Double Crossed, 68" x 68"
Paige Alexander, Easley, SC

802. Play Golf, 70" x 69"
Keiko Aso, Fukuyamashi, Hiroshima, Japan

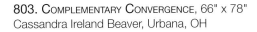

803. Complementary Convergence, 66" x 78"
Cassandra Ireland Beaver, Urbana, OH

804. Swatch, 68" x 71"
Sara Bradshaw and Danielle Johnson, Spencer, TN

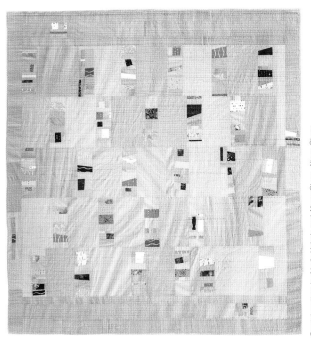

Swatch pattern by Nydia Kehnle and Alison Glass, Alison Glass

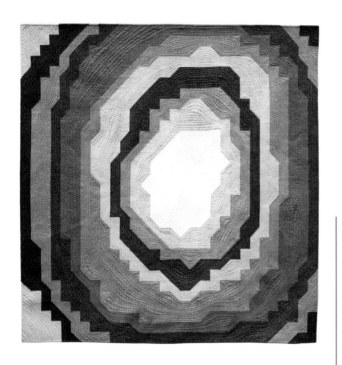

805. STONE SLICE, 60" x 60"
Sheri Cifaldi-Morrill, Woodbridge, CT

806. HEXAMETRY, 73" x 73"
Miyuki Kuwabara, Minato, Tokyo, Japan

807. BLACK STARS, 60" x 74"
Mary Lorenz, Austin, TX

808. BLACK, BROWN, AND WHITE IN ORANGE,
78" x 78"
Karen Maple, Portola Valley, CA

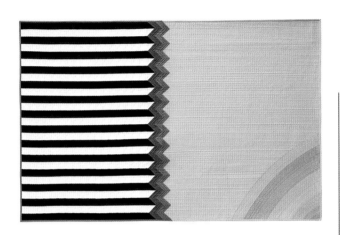

809. FINITE STRUGGLE... INFINITE HOPE, 61" x 40"
Sarah Maxwell, Mexico, MO

810. BIRD BY BIRD, 64" x 78"
Deirdre McConathy, Henderson, KY

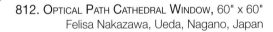

811. MIGRATION PATTERNS, 70" x 55"
Susan Mogan, Mobile, AL

812. OPTICAL PATH CATHEDRAL WINDOW, 60" x 60"
Felisa Nakazawa, Ueda, Nagano, Japan

813. VIBRATO, 62" x 42"
Carolina Oneto, Colina, Región Metropolitana, Chile

814. THE MODERN DRUNK, 60" x 53"
Jodi Robinson, Enon Valley, PA

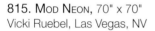

815. MOD NEON, 70" x 70"
Vicki Ruebel, Las Vegas, NV

816. JEWEL DROP, 72" x 72"
Sylvia Schaefer, Athens, GA

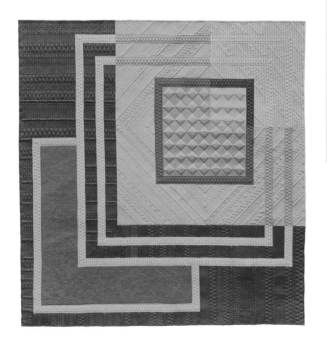

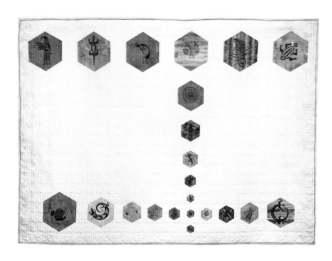

817. HISTORICALLY MODERN, 69" x 51"
Barbara Shiffler, Matthews, NC

818. MY MODERN MAY BASKET, 62" x 62"
Sherry Werum, Woodland, CA

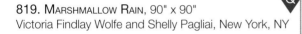

819. MARSHMALLOW RAIN, 90" x 90"
Victoria Findlay Wolfe and Shelly Pagliai, New York, NY

901. A-TEAM'S ROSE OF SHARON 1, 79" x 99"
A-Team Appliqué Group, Chesterfield, MO

Group Quilts

902. CARPETBAG, 96" x 96"
Bags and Tarts, Innishannon, Cork, Ireland

903. 2 DEGREES CELSIUS, 66" x 70"
BeeSewcial, Denver, CO

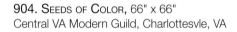

904. SEEDS OF COLOR, 66" x 66"
Central VA Modern Guild, Charlottesvle, VA

905. LILIES OF THE GUILD, 92" x 92"
Faithful Circle, Downers Grove, IL

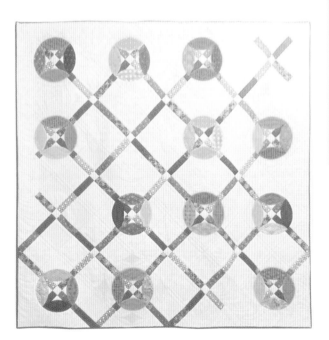

906. UMIMACHI, 85" x 85"
Fujieda North High School, Fujieda, Shizuoka, Japan

907. GENESEE VALLEY FRIENDSHIP QUILT, 91" x 91"
Genesee Valley Quilt Club, Penfield, NY

908. JOURNEY TO FRIENDSHIP, 79" x 91"
Journey Girls, Kevil, KY

909. ROSE, ROSE, AND ROSE!, 63" x 56"
Kazuyo & 8 Friends, Setagaya, Tokyo, Japan

Rose of Sharon Mix & Match Quilting Collection by Anita Goodesign and Patches of Life pattern by Eleanor Burns, Quilt in a Day

Focus on Appliqué pattern by Irene Blanck, *Quiltmania*

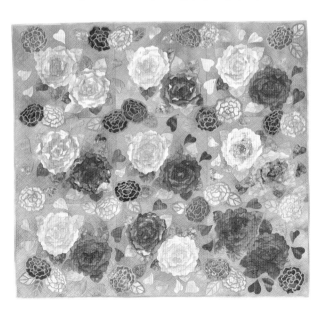

Group Quilts

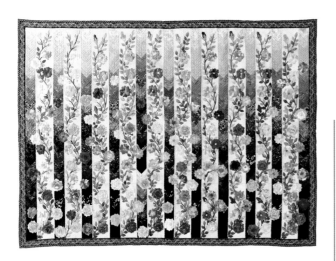

910. La Vie En Rose, 100" x 72"
Mie Yamada & 7 Amigas, Setagaya, Tokyo, Japan

911. Mala Pua (Flower Garden), 79" x 79"
Miyoko & 15 Friends, Setagaya, Tokyo, Japan

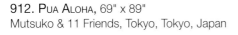

912. Pua Aloha, 69" x 89"
Mutsuko & 11 Friends, Tokyo, Tokyo, Japan

913. Farm Fresh, 68" x 82"
Naperville Modern Guild, Hinsdale, IL

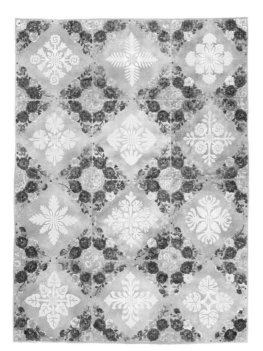

Farm Girl Vintage by Lori Holt © 2015 It's Sew Emma

914. Love Flamingo, 75" x 86"
Nobuko & 11 Friends, Setagaya, Tokyo, Japan

915. Le Jardin, 68" x 44"
PSQG Art Bee, Wayne, IL

916. Bonnie's Garden, 68" x 80"
Seven Stellar Stitchers, Paducah, KY

917. Reaching for the Stars, 80" x 96"
Shenandoah Valley Quilters Guild, Toms Brook, VA

A Primitive Garden pattern by Lisa Bongean, Primitive Gatherings

Group Quilts

918. Come Dance with Me, 75" x 75"
The Quilting Page, Apple Valley, MN

919. Sunrise in Arcadia, 70" x 70"
Third Thursday Quilters, Palestine, TX

920. Group Therapy, 65" x 75"
Waynesville Girls, Waynesville, NC

921. Klimt Nouveau, 62" x 75"
Wild FEW, Sequim, WA

Swallows in the Window pattern from *Once Upon a Season: Nine Appliquéd and Pieced Quilts, Celebrating Every Season* from *Piece O' Cake Designs* by Becky Goldsmith and Linda Jenkins © 2003 C&T Publishing, Backyard Birds pattern from *Wild Birds: Designs for Appliqué & Quilting* by Carol Armstrong © 2000 C&T Publishing, and Birds & Flowers Album by Bea Oglesby © 2003 American Quilters Society

922. CHRISTMAS HOUSE, 79" x 94"
Yoko & 8 Friends, Setagaya, Tokyo, Japan

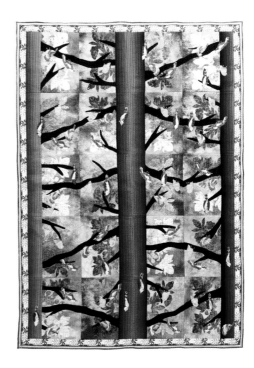

923. A GATHERING OF BIRDS, 74" x 103"
Yosuke & Osaka Friends, Setagaya, Tokyo, Japan

1001. BERRY PATCH WORK, 46" x 48"
Pam Beal, Mass City, MI

1002. HIDDEN THOUGHTS II: DAY'S END REVIEW
32" x 33"
Sue Cortese, Holland, MI

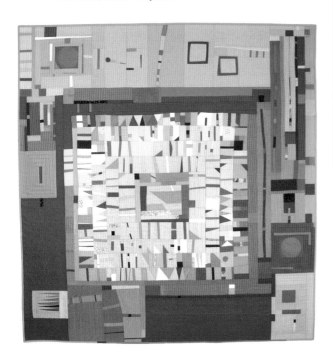

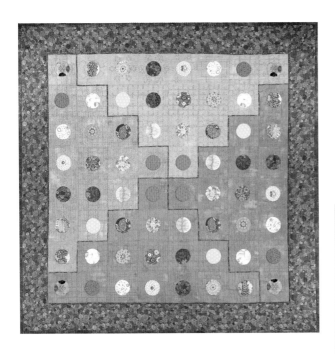

1003. THE SUM OF ODD INTEGERS, 58" x 58"
Elaine Krajenke Ellison, Sarasota, FL

Baltimore Spring pattern by Pearl P. Pereira, P3 Designs

1004. HOW DOES YOUR GARDEN GROW?, 59" x 54"
Barbara (Bobbe) Green and Gale Polk, Paducah, KY

1005. VIVACITY, 52" x 52"
Kayoko Hata, Yokohama, Kanagawa, Japan

1006. A SASHIKO STILL LIFE, 42" x 42"
Lissa LaGreca, Bexley, OH

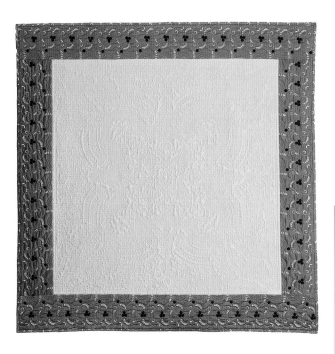

1007. GOLDEN SPLENDOR, 46" x 46"
Andi Perejda, Arroyo Grande, CA

1008. SARMIENTITE, 34" x 48"
Andrea Stracke, Groß Niendorf, Germany

1009. FLOATING LILIES ALONG THE WATER II
37" x 37"
Akemi Sugiyama, Hachioji, Tokyo, Japan

1010. LIFE OF SUNBONNET GIRLS, 59" x 58"
Michiko Takahashi, Hadano, Kanagawa, Japan

Small Wall Quilts – Hand Quilted
Small Wall Quilts – Stationary Machine Quilted

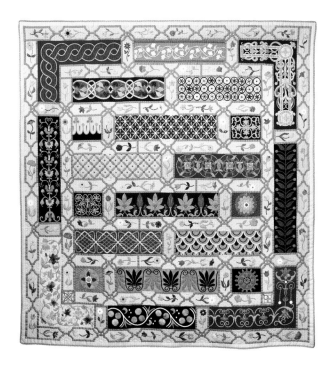

1011. For Love of Ornament, 62" x 66"
Zena Thorpe, Chatsworth, CA

1012. Sewing is Beleafing, 58" x 68"
Christine Wickert, Penfield, NY

1101. Momotaro, the Peach Boy, 57" x 57"
Keiko Aso, Fukuyamashi, Hiroshima, Japan

1102. Car Talk, 41" x 33"
Esterita Austin, Port Jefferson Station, NY

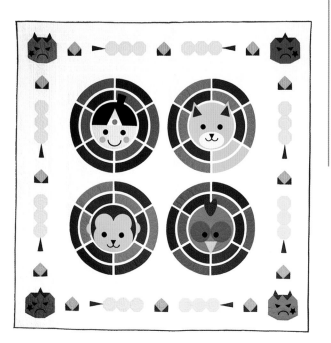

1103. GARDEN, 43" x 53"
Beth Brady, Marietta, GA

1104. BLACK AND TAN, 54" x 54"
Caryl Sloane Brix, Byron, IL

1105. TRELLIS BLOOMS, 56" x 67"
Jean Brueggenjohann, Columbia, MO

1106. PINK ACORNS, 54" x 54"
Christine Copenhaver, Boulder, CO

45 & Life To Go pattern by Lisa Bongean, Primitive Gatherings

1107. POLARIZATION PAIN, 42" x 33"
Sandy Curran, Newport News, VA

1108. MY KOI POND, 43" x 52"
Judy DenHerder, Zephyrhills, FL

1109. ADVENTURES IN WONDERLAND, 49" x 60"
Fabia Diniz, Sorocaba, São Paulo, Brazil

1110. TERRACOTTA ARMY CHARIOTS, 44" x 56"
Karen Donobedian, Waldport, OR

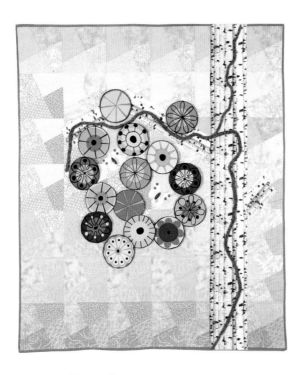

1111. FLORAL EXPLOSION, 48" x 56"
Paula B. Entin, Fairview, NC

1112. MORNING RAIN, 53" x 33"
Sarah Entsminger, Ashburn, VA

1113. MIDNIGHT FANTASY #10, 49" x 49"
Caryl Bryer Fallert-Gentry, Port Townsend, WA

1114. SIGN, SEALED, AND DELIVERED, 54" x 41"
Sheila Gaquin, Deer Harbor, WA

1115. On the Spectrum, 42" x 52"
Nikki Hill, St. Augustine, FL

1116. Antique Tiny Trip, 59" x 60"
Pat Holly, Ann Arbor, MI

1117. Ready to Dance?, 56" x 42"
Mikyung Jang, Seoul, South Korea

1118. Copper Enamel Ammonite, 35" x 49"
Kimberly Lacy, Colorado Springs, CO

Photograph by Carlos Ramírez de Arellano del Rey

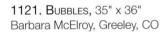

1119. LITTLE VILLAGE IN MY HEART, 53" x 50"
Sangok Lee, Seoul, South Korea

1120. RAINY DAY IN MADRID, 43" x 60"
Marisa Marquez, Aurora, IL

1121. BUBBLES, 35" x 36"
Barbara McElroy, Greeley, CO

1122. RAINBOW ROADS, 41" x 56"
Isabel Muñoz, Madrid, Spain

1123. TICKLED PINK, 56" x 56"
Sharon Murphy and Georgianne Kandler, Renton, WA

1124. FRANCIS BAY, 34" x 40"
Jean Overmeyer, Monroe, MI

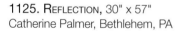

1125. REFLECTION, 30" x 57"
Catherine Palmer, Bethlehem, PA

1126. CRANBERRY BOUNCE, 53" x 54"
Ann L. Petersen, Surprise, AZ

1127. SEASONS OF MY GARDEN, 36" x 36"
Elaine Ross, Batavia, NY

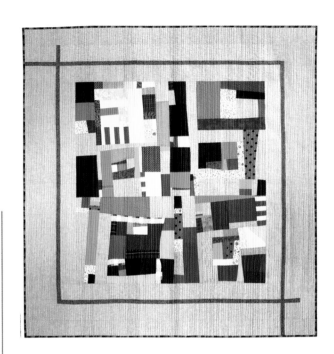

1128. BRACKETED, 52" x 52"
Stephanie Zacharer Ruyle, Denver, CO

1129. PROTECTING THE FLAME, 39" x 37"
Sandi Snow, Lutz, FL

1130. FULL BLOWN, 53" x 37"
Nancy Sterett Martin, Owensboro, KY

1131. RACE TO THE SUMMIT, 44" x 30"
Brigitte Villeneuve, Jonquière, Quebec, Canada

1132. LOYAL, 30" x 30"
Chi Chen Wen, Ping Tung, Taiwan

1133. GARDEN VARIETY, 40" x 40"
Geraldine Wilkins, Fredericksburg, VA

1134. DRAGONS NAVIGATING THE COSMOS, 33" x 33"
Linda Woodard, Marion, IL

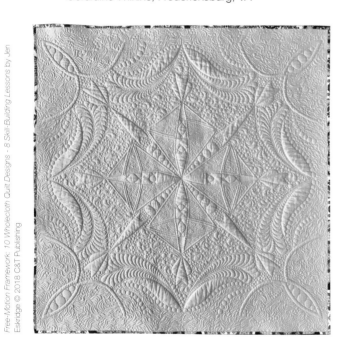

Free-Motion Framework: 10 Wholecloth Quilt Designs - 8 Skill-Building Lessons by Jen Eskridge © 2018 C&T Publishing

Persian Star pattern from WedgeWorks by Cheryl Phillips © 1997 Phillips Fiber Art

1201. SUNFLOWER, 60" x 53"
Sara Bradshaw and Danielle Johnson, Spencer, TN

1202. GOLDEN GALAXY, 50" x 50"
Aline Bugarin and Natasha Bugarin
Campinas, São Paulo, Brazil

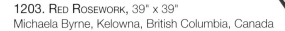

1203. RED ROSEWORK, 39" x 39"
Michaela Byrne, Kelowna, British Columbia, Canada

1204. SEE THE LEAVES FOR THE TREE, 58" x 78"
Marilyn Farquhar, Heidelberg, Ontario, Canada

The Raven: An Autumn Quilt of 9 Appliqué Designs by Alma Allen and Barb Adams © 2016 Blackbird Designs

1205. AFTERNOONS WITH THE FAUNS, 53" x 54"
Trina Freshour and Ruth Gevers, Lebanon, IL

1206. THE RAVEN, 50" x 50"
Barbara (Bobbe) Green and Terry Russelburg
Paducah, KY

1207. PERSISTENCE, 40" x 40"
Margaret Solomon Gunn, Gorham, ME

1208. DUAL SPIRALS, 42" x 39"
Jessica Harper, Hurst, TX

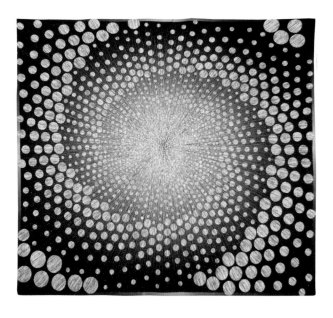

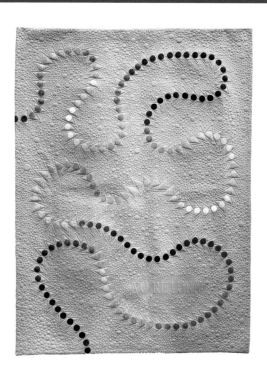

1209. CIRCLING THE RAINBOW, 51" x 62"
Julie Kennedy and Janice Walsh, College Park, GA

1210. NO RETURN, 35" x 47"
Anne Lillholm, Nuenen, Noord-Brabant, Netherlands

1211. ALL ROADS LEAD HOME, 48" x 48"
Ann Matheson, Mount Dora, FL

1212. GREY OMBRE, 54" x 54"
Wilma Moss and Floyd Moss, Sulphur Springs, TX

1213. BUBBLE BALLET, 40" x 42"
Birgit Schüeller, Riegelsberg, Germany

1214. TIC-TAC-OH!, 50" x 50"
Maria Shell, Anchorage, AK

1215. AMERICAN ALBUM, 58" x 58"
Kathy Shier, Apple Valley, MN

1216. FELICITOUS PICKLE, 52" x 68"
Kelly Spell, Hixson, TN

American Album block series by Pearl P. Pereira, P3 Designs

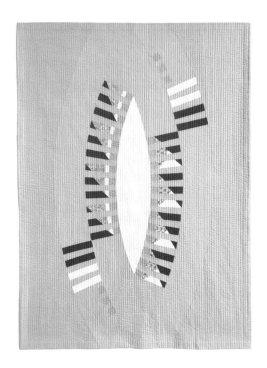

Stack-n-Whack® pattern by Bethany Reynolds

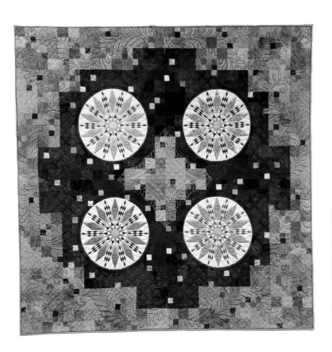

Night Sky pattern by Julie Herman, Jaybird Quilts

1217. MAGNETIC ATTRACTION, 54" x 54"
Gail Stepanek and Jan Hutchison, New Lenox, IL

1218. NIGHT SKY, 55" x 64"
Jackie Van Houten, Monroe, MI

1301. HOLIDAY HOUSES, 46" x 70"
Jan Lee Asmann, Okemos, MI

1302. AUTO ARACHNID, 42" x 53"
Esterita Austin, Port Jefferson Station, NY

Holiday Houses appliqué patterns by Debra Gabel, zebrapatterns.com

Bowtie Ben by Punch Studio

1303. RAFA, 39" x 48"
Marcia Baraldi and Valeria Baraldi
Florianopolis, Santa Catarina, Brazil

1304. CROSSING THE BRAZOS, 50" x 54"
Judy Beskow, College Station, TX

1305. DANCE OF THE TWIRLY GIRLS, 40" x 53"
Andrea Brokenshire, Round Rock, TX

1306. INDIGO AFTERNOON, 30" x 41"
Amy Cavaness, Marseilles, IL

1307. SASHA AND CHANEL, 35" x 42"
Amanda Clark, Fort Collins, CO

1308. CHICKEN RUN, 52" x 47"
Halime Conger, Barrington, IL

1309. ON THIN ICE, 48" x 35"
Deb Crine, Marco Island, FL

1310. RAIN, 31" x 56"
Sandy Curran, Newport News, VA

Photograph from Pixabay

1311. UNTITLED, 34" x 36"
Lynn Czaban, Eugene, OR

1312. MAJESTIC PRESENCE, 36" x 42"
Sue de Vanny, Greenvale, Victoria, Australia

1313. WOLF—THE EYES HAVE IT, 40" x 30"
Rhonda S. Denney, Canon City, CO

1314. 1955, 45" x 37"
Carol Dickson, Cave Junction, OR

1315. Jack, 52" x 71"
Marilyn Farquhar, Heidelberg, Ontario, Canada

1316. Wild, 44" x 30"
Laura Fogg, Ukiah, CA

1317. The Gate, 36" x 31"
Irene M. Foss, Bella Vista, AR

1318. Bearded Man with a Pencil, 30" x 35"
Rita Gazubey, Kiev, Ukraine

Photograph of the Lake District, England and *Snippet Sensations: Fast, Fusible Fabric Art for Quilted or Framed Projects* by Cindy Walter © 1999 Krause Publications

1319. THE NARROWS, 31" x 37"
Cathy Geier, Waukesha, WI

Phenomenal Women by Margaret Warfield

1320. PHENOMENAL WOMEN, 34" x 39"
Rebecca Ann Haley, Porterville, CA

1321. VIRGINIA CITY MINER, 50" x 68"
LeAnn Hileman, Glendale, AZ

1322. FACES IN THE DARK, 60" x 60"
Patricia Kennedy-Zafred, Murrysville, PA

Photos from Library of Congress, Farm Security Administration Collection, US National Archives, Bituminous Coal Industry Collection

1323. An Old Woman with Joyous Face, 49" x 70"
Marina Landi, São Paulo, São Paulo, Brazil

1324. Jangdokdae—The Mother's Space, 40" x 51"
Eunhee Lee, Seoul, South Korea

1325. Dad's Blue Truck, 40" x 35"
Tonya Littmann, Denton, TX

1326. Wisconsin Road Trip, 48" x 38"
Sally Manke, Arcadia, MI

1327. Spring Harmony, 48" x 52"
Kathy McNeil, Tulalip, WA

1328. Samba Selfie, 39" x 39"
Randa Mulford, Mountain View, CA

1329. Autumn in Sankyoson, 60" x 48"
Kyoko Oura, Nanto, Toyama, Japan

1330. An Ordinary Day, 30" x 50"
Susan V. Polansky, Lexington, MA

1331. Is She Ready Yet?, 58" x 55"
Heidi Proffetty, Bridgewater, MA

1332. Intense Patience, 37" x 34"
Jody H. Rusconi, McKinleyville, CA

1333. Huddle!, 50" x 32"
Sue Sherman, Newmarket, Ontario, Canada

1334. Frosted Idaho Pines, 48" x 55"
Karen H. Sienk, Colden, NY

1335. Loving Amsterdam, 52" x 37"
Jan Soules, Elk Grove, CA

1336. Beautiful Smile, 46" x 58"
Sasiwimol Sujit, Yasothon, Thailand

1337. Goat in a Coat, 37" x 48"
Sue Turnquist, Crawfordville, FL

1338. Sunset at Camel Rock, 34" x 42"
Angie Tustison, McKinleyville, CA

1401. COWGIRLS, 38" x 34"
Margaret Abramshe, St. George, UT

1402. TIME WARP, 55" x 50"
Guner Ata, Ankara, Turkey

1403. ABBEY'S FLOWER GARDEN, 63" x 63"
Ceidys Butterworth, Frisco, TX

1404. PLAYING IN THE WATERFALL, 57" x 41"
Valeria Cervetto, São Paulo, São Paulo, Brazil

Forget Me Not Sew Along by Sue Daley, Sue Daley Designs

Water war photograph by Rarindra Prakarsa

Meringue Mix by Wayne Thiebaud © 1989

End of the Trail by Michael J. Meketi © 1970

1405. Meringue Pies, 30" x 43"
Karen N. Crocker, Waukesha, WI

1406. End of the Trail, 49" x 50"
Jane A. Deskis, Leavenworth, KS

1407. Shimmering Radiance, 74" x 74"
Mary Dillman, Woodlawn, IL

1408. Refraction, 52" x 70"
Megan Ellinger, Spring Hill, TN

Spring Garden pattern by Cheryl Malkowski, cheryl rose creations

1409. ISLAMIC ART, 59" x 59"
Faiza Elmayergi
White Rock, British Columbia, Canada

1410. SUNSTRUCK, 49" x 49"
Ginny Flock and Barb Jolley, Deerfield, IL

1411. HAND IN HAND, 83" x 83"
Taeko Ito, Ogaki, Gifu, Japan

1412. AFTER A WINTER STORM, 45" x 59"
Patsy Kittredge, Sedona, AZ

Ricky Tims' Kool Kaleidoscope Quilts: Simple Strip-Piecing Technique for Stunning Results by Ricky Tims © 2010 C&T Publishing

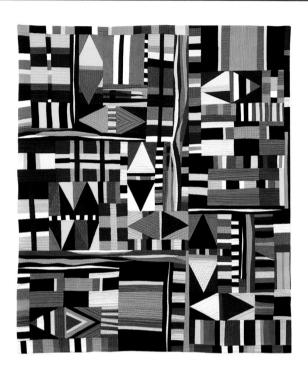

1413. Geometric Primary, 33" x 36"
Michele Lea, Oxford, OH

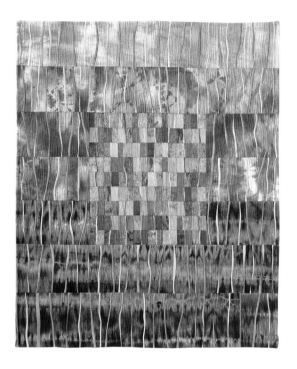

1414. Waiting for Spring, 37" x 44"
Eunhee Lee, Seoul, South Korea

1415. Blue Moon, 30" x 30"
Mary Lorenz, Austin, TX

1416. August Oklahoma Prairie, 56" x 59"
Megan Lundgren, Minco, OK

Pickle Promenade pattern by Sharon Schamber, Sharon Master Quilter

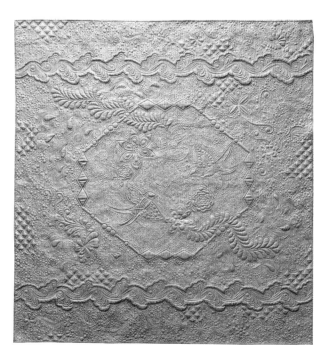

1417. HAPPINESS IN MY CABIN, 41" x 41"
Laurie Miller, Rolla, MO

1418. TWO SOCKS, 43" x 54"
Natalie Mosher, London, AR

1419. SUNNY PLACE, 56" x 56"
Masayo Niimi, Kasugai, Aichi, Japan

1420. WARLIGHT, 70" x 70"
Julie Parrish, Henderson, NV

1421. FLOWER GIRL, 31" x 39"
Ellen Parrott, Dansville, MI

1422. BOBBIN LACE, 51" x 51"
Joana Pegado, Rio de Janeiro, Rio de Janeiro, Brazil

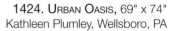

1423. MULTNOMAH FALLS, 38" x 58"
Judy Peterson, Eugene, OR

1424. URBAN OASIS, 69" x 74"
Kathleen Plumley, Wellsboro, PA

Multnomah Falls photograph by Angelia Peterson, Nod to Nature

A Walk in the Meadow pattern by Ellen Heck

1425. A Walk in the Meadow, 51" x 51"
Debby Porter and Alicia Edwards, Casper, WY

1427. Berrylicious, 48" x 40"
Joanne Hannon Shaw, Toronto, Ontario, Canada

Photograph by Georgina Steytler and photograph by Celine Dubois

1426. Endangered Flight Path:
Destination Unknown, 39" x 39"
Julie Psarras, Drouin, Victoria, Australia

1428. SPLAT!, 67" x 77"
Dawn Siden, Somers, MT

Photograph by Joel Davidson

Raindrops pattern by Judy and Bradley Niemeyer, Quiltworx.com

WPAP (Wedha's Pop Art Portrait) image of Lincoln by Ihsan Ekaputra

1429. LINCOLN, 46" x 60"
Kim Smith Soper, Huntington, NY

1430. ENCOUNTER FLOWERS, 71" x 71"
Mariko Tachikawa, Inasawa, Aichi, Japan

1431. CAT RHYTHM, 35" x 30"
Chi Chen Wen, Ping Tung, Taiwan

1432. ABUNDANCE, 53" x 53"
Geraldine Wilkins, Fredericksburg, VA

1501. The Jump, 33" x 62"
Cristina Arcenegui Bono, Alcalá de Guadaíra, Spain

1502. Sundown / Cedar Key, 60" x 55"
Peggy Brown, Nashville, IN

1503. Chameleon—The Eyes Have It, 40" x 30"
Rhonda S. Denney, Canon City, CO

1504. Dot Almighty, 40" x 40"
Carol D. Duffy, Plymouth, MA

1505. A WINTER'S MORNING, 52" x 36"
Sarah Entsminger, Ashburn, VA

1506. UNSUSTAINABLE, 41" x 44"
Connie Kincius Griner, Burlington, NC

1507. CARNIVAL, 38" x 38"
Barbara Oliver Hartman, Flower Mound, TX

1508. FANCY TRIP AROUND THE WORLD, 36" x 36"
Pat Holly, Ann Arbor, MI

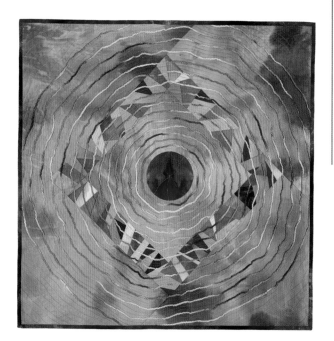

1509. ANTELOPE CANYON MOSAIC II, 51" x 41"
Kimberly Lacy, Colorado Springs, CO

1510. 60 DEGREES OF SEPARATION, 36" x 52"
Mackenzie Leake, Stanford, CA

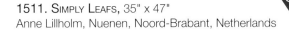

1511. SIMPLY LEAFS, 35" x 47"
Anne Lillholm, Nuenen, Noord-Brabant, Netherlands

1512. CIRC TOUCHE, 35" x 46"
Jackie Perry, Marion, VA

1513. Shadows of the Divine, 45" x 32"
Susan V. Polansky, Lexington, MA

1514. Plain and Simple, 48" x 58"
Jodi Robinson, Enon Valley, PA

1515. Torii, 42" x 47"
Stephanie Zacharer Ruyle, Denver, CO

1516. Ocean's Edge, 51" x 40"
Beth Schillig, Columbus, OH

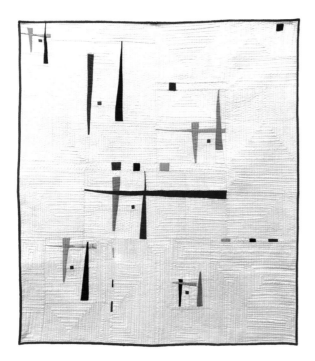

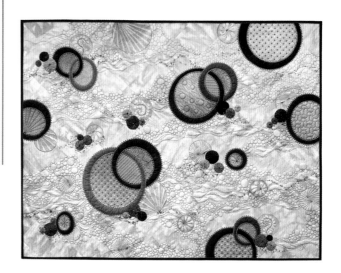

1517. THE SPRINTER, 80" x 38"
Birgit Schüeller, Riegelsberg, Germany

1518. FLOWER HAT JELLY, 41" x 43"
Kelly Spell, Hixson, TN

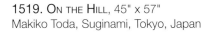

1519. ON THE HILL, 45" x 57"
Makiko Toda, Suginami, Tokyo, Japan

1520. ICY INDIANA, 31" x 41"
Barbara Triscari, Lebanon, IN

1521. DREAM HOUSES 3, 41" x 33"
Karen Turnbull, Laguna Niguel, CA

1601. SYNTHESIZED SLIVERS, 22" x 19"
Cassandra Ireland Beaver, Urbana, OH

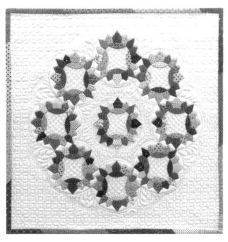

1602. ITTY BITTY BRIMFIELD, 15" x 15"
Elaine Braun, Paducah, KY

1603. I LOVE LUCY, 22" x 22"
Kay Donges, Blairsville, GA

1604. BEACH LIFE, 19" x 17"
Barb Egbert, Cape Girardeau, MO

Life's A Beach pattern by Cynthia England, England Design Studios

1605. TWISTING RIBBONS, 12" x 12"
Sharon Engel, Greeley, CO

Dancing Ribbons pattern by Cindy Rounds Richards

Trip Around the World pattern by Eleanor Burns, Quilt in a Day

1606. Dynamo, 18" x 19"
Megan Farkas, Sanbornton, NH

1607. Secret in the Garden, 15" x 15"
Kumiko Frydl, Houston, TX

1608. Lily Anna on the Highest Rock, 24" x 17"
Vicki Hastings, Rockford, IL

Photograph by Sue Benner

1609. The Sunbathers, 12" x 12"
Sue Holdaway-Heys, Ann Arbor, MI

1610. Roman Bath, 9" x 9"
Miyuki Humphries, Tokyo, Tokyo, Japan

1611. Hibiscus Bouquet, 11" x 11"
Naomi Iida, Itabashi, Tokyo, Japan

Miniature Quilts

1612. ROUTT COUNTY, Colorado, 24" x 17"
Carol A. Lang, Liberty Township, OH

1613. PLAYTIME, 15" x 15"
Joanne Love, Whitehorse, Yukon, Canada

Shattered Miniature Lone Star pattern by Paula Golden and border designed by Shirley Liby

1614. SHATTERED ARCTURUS, 20" x 20"
Mary Mahoney, Tampa, FL

1615. ANY SCRAP WILL DO, 15" x 15"
Carolyn Bucklin Mullins, Daniels, WV

1616. CIRCUIT TRAINING, 11" x 11"
Philippa Naylor, Beverley East Yorkshire,
East Riding of Yorkshire, United Kingdom

Inspired by Ricky Tims' Rhapsody Quilt methods

1617. PLEASURES AND PASSIONS—BORN UNDER WET SIGNS III,
23" x 23", Annedore Neumann, Moenchengladbach-Wickrath,
North Rhine-Westphalia, Germany

1618. TIGHT PINEAPPLE, 12" x 12"
Amy Pabst, Le Roy, WV

1619. OH, MY STARS!, 18" x 20"
Joyce Puffinbarger, Symsonia, KY

1620. LAS VEGAS POOL PARTY WITH FERNANDO
15" x 18", Annie M. Romero, North Las Vegas, NV

1621. GHOST TOWN OF ST. ELMO, 13" x 11"
Sharon L. Schlotzhauer, Monument, CO

1622. SPRING SONG, 17" x 20"
Pam Seaberg, Kenmore, WA

1623. PLUMERIA OF KOKO CRATER, 19" x 19"
Sue Sherman, Newmarket, Ontario, Canada

Miniature Quilts

1624. WONDERFUL TIME, 14" x 14"
Chiharu Takahashi, Chofu, Tokyo, Japan

1625. QUATRE COEURS, 12" x 12"
Dana Thelen, San Rafael, CA

Index of Quiltmakers

Index of Quiltmakers

Index of Quilts

Index of Quilts

2019 AQS QuiltWeek® Spring Paducah Sponsors

AQS presents the sponsors for the 35th Annual AQS QuiltWeek – Spring Paducah 2019. Each category and event is sponsored by a company in the quilting industry. Company representatives will present the cash awards at the Awards Presentation on Tuesday evening, April 23, 2019.

Best of Show . . . . **Janome America**

Best Hand Workmanship . . . . **American Quilter's Society**

Best Stationary Machine Workmanship . . . . **BERNINA of America**

Best Movable Machine Workmanship . . . . **American Professional Quilting Systems (APQS)**

Best Wall Quilt . . . . **Hobbs Bonded Fibers**

Best Wall Hand Workmanship . . . . **Coats & Clark**

Best Wall Stationary Machine Workmanship . . . . **Brother International Corporation**

Best Wall Movable Machine Workmanship . . . . **Handi Quilter**

Best Miniature Quilt . . . . **AccuQuilt**

Large Quilts, Stationary Machine Quilted . . . . **Husqvarna Viking / Sew-A-Lot**

Large Quilts, Movable Machine Quilted . . . . **Locksmith Lizzie**

Large Quilts, 1st Entry in an AQS Paducah Contest . . . . **Gammill Quilting Machines**

Large Quilts, Hand Quilted Quilts . . . . **Rotary Club of Paducah**

Wall Quilts, Stationary Machine Quilted . . . . **Baby Lock USA**

Wall Quilts, Movable Machine Quilted . . . . **Juki America, Inc.**

Wall Quilts, Pictorial . . . . **Elna USA**

Wall Quilts, Modern . . . . **Statler by Gammill**

Group Quilts . . . . **ABM International**

Small Wall Quilts, Hand Quilted . . . . **Martelli Enterprises**

Small Wall Quilts, Stationary Machine Quilted . . . . **Koala Cabinets**

Small Wall Quilts, Movable Machine Quilted . . . . **Pro-Stitcher**

Small Wall Quilts, Pictorial . . . . **Pfaff / Sew-A-Lot**

Small Wall Quilts, 1st Entry in an AQS Paducah Contest . . . . . **Horn of America**

Small Wall Quilts, Quilter's Choice . . . . **Superior Threads**

Miniature . . . . **Baby Lock Crown Jewel and Tiara**

Nancy Ann Sobel Award of Merit in Hand Quilting . . . . **The Sobel Family**

Judges' Recognition . . . . **BERNINA of America Q Series–Longarm**

Viewers' Choice . . . . **Country Heritage Tours**

General Show Sponsors . . . . **Martelli Enterprises; Quilt Path by APQS**

2019 Quilters Grand Giveaway . . . . **AccuQuilt; Janome America;**
. . . . **Quilt Seminars at Sea/Holland America Line®;**
. . . . **Opulent Quilt Journeys; ShopAQS.com;**
. . . . **WonderFil Specialty Threads**

Special Exhibit Sponsors . . . . **A-1 Quilting Machines:** *Ordinary Quilts,*
Extraordinary Quilting by Judi Madsen;
. . . . **APQS:** *Quilts of Valor Service Recognition Exhibit;*
. . . . **Brother International:** *New Quilts From an Old Favorite: Bow Tie;*
. . . . **Innova:** *Cherrywood Challenge 2018: Prince Tribute;*
. . . . **Janome America:** *The 14th Quilt Nihon Exhibition;*
. . . . **PAAQT:** *Fresh Faces/New Ideas Quilt Challenge;*
. . . . **WonderFil Specialty Threads:** *Singular Stars:*
Lone Star Quilts from Judy Martin

Workshops . . . . **AccuQuilt; BERNINA of America; Elna USA;**
. . . . **Handi Quilter; Hobbs Bonded Fibers;**
. . . . **Janome America; Juki America, Inc. /**
. . . . **SewingMachine.com; Microsun Lamps;**
. . . . **Pfaff / Sew-A-Lot; Reliable Irons;**
. . . . **WonderFil Specialty Threads**

The National Quilt Museum Education Sponsors . . . . **Janome America; Moda Fabrics**

The National Quilt Museum New Quilts from an Old Favorite . . **Janome America; Moda Fabrics**

School Block Challenge . . . . **Moda Fabrics**

35
YEARS
AQS Quilt Show
Best of Show Winners
1985–2018

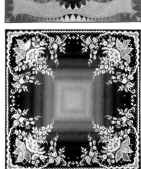

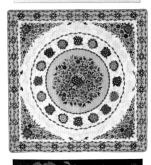

AQS Quilt Show Best of Show Winners
1985–2018

1985 AQS Best of Show
ORIENTAL FANTASY, 82" x 98"
Katherine E. Inman, Brecksville, OH

1986 AQS Best of Show
SPRING WINDS, 76" x 87"
Faye Anderson, Denver, CO

1987 AQS Best of Show
AUTUMN RADIANCE, 81" x 93"
Sharon Rauba, Woodridge, IL

1988 AQS Best of Show
GYPSY IN MY SOUL, 66" x 84"
Jane Blair, Conshohocken, PA

1989 AQS Best of Show
CORONA II: SOLAR ECLIPSE, 76" x 94"
Carol Bryer Fallert, Oswego, IL

1990 AQS Best of Show
THE BEGINNINGS, 64" x 84"
Dawn E. Amos, Rapid City, SD

1991 AQS Best of Show
DAWN SPLENDOR, 94" x 94"
Nancy Ann Sobel, Brooktondale, NY

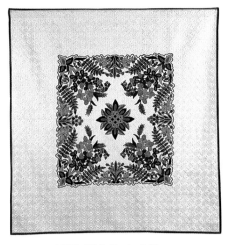

1992 AQS Best of Show
MOMMA'S GARDEN, 88" x 91"
Anne Oliver, Alexandria, VA

1993 AQS Best of Show
AIR SHOW, 81" X 81"
Jonathan Shannon, Belvedere, CA

1994 AQS Best of Show
WILD ROSE, 90" x 90"
Fay Pritts, Mt. Pleasant, PA

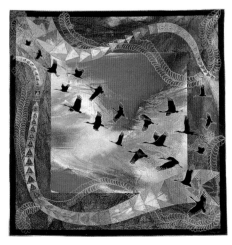

1995 AQS Best of Show
MIGRATION #2, 88" x 88"
Carol Bryer Fallert, Oswego, IL

1996 AQS Best of Show
AUBUSSON JARDEN PARTIERE, 81" x 90"
Betty Ekern Suiter, Racine, WI

AQS Quilt Show Best of Show Winners
1985–2018

1997 AQS Best of Show
VINTAGE ROSE GARDEN, 94" x 94.5"
Judith Thompson, Wenonah, NJ

1998 AQS Best of Show
THE BEATLES QUILT, 95" x 95"
Pat Holly, Muskegon, MI and
Sue Nickels, Ann Arbor, MI

1999 Hancock's of Paducah Best of Show
JOIE DE VIE – JOY OF LIFE, 94" x 94"
Candy Goff, Lolo, MT

2000 Hancock's of Paducah Best of Show
BIRDS OF A DIFFERENT COLOR, 74" x 93"
Carol Bryer Fallert, Oswego, IL

2001 Hancock's of Paducah Best of Show
KELLS: MAGNUM OPUS, 81" x 90"
Zena Thorpe, Chatsworth, CA

2002 Hancock's of Paducah Best of Show
WELCOME TO MY DREAMS, 79.5" x 86.5"
Betty Ekern Suiter, Racine, WI

2003 Hancock's of Paducah Best of Show
LIME LIGHT, 81" x 81"
Philippa Naylor, Dhahran, Saudi Arabia

2004 Hancock's of Paducah Best of Show
SPICE OF LIFE, 82" x 82"
Linda M. Roy, Pittsfield, MA

2005 Hancock's of Paducah Best of Show
BIRDS 'N' ROSES, 83" x 84"
Margaret Docherty, Broompark, Durham, U.K.

2006 AQS Best of Show
SEDONA ROSE, 105" x 110"
Sharon Schamber, Payson, AZ

2007 Janome America Best of Show
FLOWER OF LIFE, 87" x 87"
Sharon Schamber, Payson, AZ

2008 Janome America Best of Show
SPRING OF DESIRE, 80" x 80"
Ted Storm-van Weelden, 's-Gravenzande,
Zuid-Holland, Netherlands

2009 Janome America Best of Show
RENAISSANCE REVIVAL, 86½" x 86½"
Mariya Waters, Melbourne, Victoria, Australia

2010 Janome America Best of Show
TRIBUTE TO TOLKIEN, 85" x 90"
Sue McCarty, Roy UT

2011 Janome America Best of Show
PAISLEY PEACOCK, 60" x 72"
Pat Holly, Ann Arbor, MI

2012 Janome America Best of Show
HARMONY WITHIN, 71" x 81"
Sue McCarty, Roy UT

2013 Janome America Best of Show
FIESTA MEXICO, 85" x 90"
Renae Haddadin and Karen Kay Buckley, Sandy UT

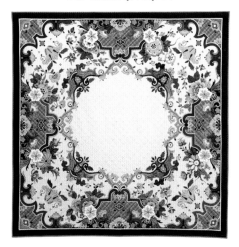

2014 Janome America Best of Show
ELaTED, 89" x 89"
Ted Storm, 's-Gravenzande, Zuid-Holland,
Netherlands

2015 Janome America Best of Show
MAJESTIC MOSAIC, 86" x 86"
Karen Kay Buckley and Renae Haddadin, Carlisle, PA

2016 Janome America Best of Show
ARANDANO, 76" x 76"
Marilyn Badger, St. George, UT

2017 Janome America Best of Show
EWE ARE MY SUNSHINE, 63" x 72"
Janet Stone, Overland Park, KS

2018 Janome America Best of Show
TURKISH TREASURES, 67" x 73"
Pat Holly, Ann Arbor, MI

Note: Name, city, and state at time of entry is listed for these winners.

AQS Quilt Show • 1985–2019

By the numbers…

$25,462,149 economic impact on the regional area in 2014

$5,836,900 in prize money has been given away by AQS

$3,282,400 has been awarded in prize money at the Paducah Quilt Shows 1985–2019

$463,250 total prize money will be given to AQS Quilt Contest winners in 2019

$126,000 in cash awards at the Spring Paducah Show 2019

31,000+ in attendance at the Spring Paducah Show

600+ quilts for viewing at AQS QuiltWeek in Paducah

300 volunteers, AQS employees, and quilt enthusiasts help AQS put on the show

44 states and 16 countries have quilts juried into the 2019 Spring Paducah Show

44 states and 8 countries have people registered for classes at the Spring Paducah Show

5 days of setup and build-in for AQS QuiltWeek in Paducah

2 days for judges to critique and pick award winners

1 terrific quilting experience in Quilt City USA®

Trivia

AQS was the 1st quilt show to award $10,000 (1985) and then $20,000 (2004) for Best of Show.

The first AQS Best of Show winner was Katherine Inman with her quilt, ORIENTAL FANTASY, in 1985.

The first machine-quilted quilt to win a major award at a quilt show: Caryl Bryer Fallert won the AQS Best of Show award in 1989 with her quilt, CORONA II: SOLAR ECLIPSE.

The first quilt that was longarm machine quilted to win a major award: Sharon Schamber won the AQS Best of Show in 2006 with her quilt, SEDONA ROSE.

Caryl Bryer Fallert-Gentry has won three Best of Show awards: the AQS Best of Show awards in 1989 and 1995 and the Hancock's of Paducah Best of Show award in 2000.

Renae Haddadin and Karen Kay Buckley won two Janome America Best of Show awards, in 2013 and 2015.

Pat Holly won two Janome America Best of Show awards, in 2011 and 2018. Pat and her sister, Sue Nickels, won the AQS Best of Show award in 1998.

Sue McCarty won two Janome America Best of Show awards, in 2010 and 2012.

Sharon Schamber is the only quilter to win two consecutive AQS Best of Show awards, in 2006 and 2007.

Ted Storm won two Janome America Best of Show awards, in 2008 and 2014.

Betty Ekhern Suiter won the AQS Best of Show award in 1996 and the Hancock's of Paducah Best of Show award in 2002.

In 2011, the entire show had to be moved due to high water and installation of the floodgates along the Ohio River. Classes were held at the First Baptist Church, and vacant buildings at Kentucky Oaks Mall housed vendors and quilts along with the Dome Pavilion, which was on the city side of the floodwall.

The first Longarm award was given in 2002, sponsored by Gammill.

The Hobbs Bonded Fibers Fashion Show was held for 20 years, from 1987 to 2006.

AQS used the new Carson Center for the Performing Arts for the first time in 2004 for the Awards Presentation.

The Dome Pavilion was first used in 2010 for vendors and special quilt exhibits.